Ernest Hemingway

A Brief Biography from Beginning to the End

The Biography

History Hub

Get Free Books for Top
Kindle Promos

Never run out of free books in your favorite genre.

CONTENTS

Part One: Editor Foreword

"Those who don't know history are doomed to repeat it." — Edmund Burke
More than ever, it is important that we equip ourselves with the power of knowledge to learn from the lessons of mistakes from the past to ensure that we do not fall victim to similar mistakes. It is our aim to provide quality history books for readers to learn important history lessons critical for everyone. And we'd like to make sure you learn the stories faster, and more efficiently.

This is why we are constantly updating our catalog with new releases in History Hub. You can access the catalog of all the new titles here. Thanks for reading, History Hub

Attention: Get Your Free Gift Now

Every <u>purchase</u> now comes with a FREE Bonus Gift

2020 Top 5 Fireside Books of the Year
(New-York Times Bestsellers, USA Today & more)

Chapter One: A Life from Beginning to End

Did You Know?

The term "Lost Generation" refers to the generational cohort after the first World War. The word "lost" connotes the "disoriented, wandering, and directionless" spirit of war survivors. Ernest Hemingway popularized it in his book, The Sun Also Rises, published in 1926.

†††

The year 1899 is when America participated in many small-scale wars overseas that resulted in peace treaties in Spain and Paris. War, in itself, could be the reason for a variety of events to happen. Once America won, Americans celebrated and mourned for deaths of thousands of soldiers and civilians, and the country acquired several new territories after Spain ceded them. The same year, a baby was born that would soon shape American literature in the most significant ways by translating the realities of war into stories of survival, hope, and celebrating humanity.

Ernest Hemingway was born into a family of 8, whose mother didn't want to be bound by the restrictions of gender norms. She would often dress her children the way she wanted, with Ernest often wearing feminine clothes. During high school, Hemingway already showed a promising future for literature–he was a journalist for the school newspaper Trapeze and their yearbook Tabula.

In 1917, Hemingway completed his secondary education–the same year when the United States was preparing for the First World War against the Central Powers of Germany, Austria, Hungary, Bulgaria, and the Ottoman Empire. Every able-bodied man was allowed to join the American forces for the war, and Hemingway was no exception. However, his dreams of serving the military were forced to a halt when the United States Army rejected him because of poor eyesight. Unwilling to give up, Hemingway found himself signed as a Red Cross recruit, who would soon be deployed as an ambulance driver in Italy for the war. The following year, he arrived in Paris when the city was bombarded by German artillery. Hemingway arrived in Italy in June, where he was immediately sent to the war zone to retrieve the bodies of fallen comrades. Days after, he was not spared from serious injury when he was wounded by mortar fire while on duty.

Hemingway was brought to the hospital, where he recuperated for six months. In the hospital, he met and fell in love with Agnes von Kurowsky, a Red Cross nurse seven years older than him. But she rejected him for another man, devastating and deeply wounding Hemingway. In 1919, he returned to America and continued his recovery. After recuperating, Hemingway landed a job as a WWI correspondent for the Toronto Star. He traveled to Paris, where he met famous American writers Gertrude Stein, Ezra Pound, and F. Scott Fitzgerald, influencing him to be a novelist.

As a driver and a journalist, his experiences with war were enough for Hemingway to share what truly happened on the battlefield. In 1924, he published his first book, In Our Time, a collection of stories about the war struggles. The following year, it was released in New York. In 1925, Hemingway cemented his name among the famous novelists at the time when he published The Sun Also Rises. The book earned him the fame which he both wanted and hated for the rest of his life. The same year, he published The Torrents of Spring, a parody to Sherwood Anderson's Dark Laughter. In 1929, Hemingway released A Farewell to Arms, yet another critical acclaim and his first bestseller. Hemingway wrote more books since then–most were set with war as the backdrop, given his wartime expertise.

In 1928, Hemingway's family departed France and returned to the United States after suffering a severe injury in their residence's bathroom. The incident left a prominent scar on his forehead, which he carried until the last day of his life. While traveling to Florida, he received the shocking news that his father had killed himself. Hemingway spent the early 1930s in his residences at Key West in winters and Wyoming in summers. In 1933, together with his wife, he took a 10-week trip to Kenya. The safari served as the material for the short stories The Snows of Kilimanjaro and The Short Happy Life of Francis Macomber, which Hemingway compiled in his book, Green Hills of Africa.

In 1939 and 1944, Hemingway returned to the warzone to cover the Spanish Civil War and the Second World War. During this time, he worked on pieces that would contribute more to his critically acclaimed status, such as For Whom the Bell Tolls. However, from 1946 onwards, Hemingway's depression had gotten worse due to several unfortunate events in his family. Additionally, many of his literary friends began to die. His injuries were also giving him recurring pain. These, however, didn't stop him from winning the Pulitzer Prize in 1952 for The Old Man and the Sea and Nobel Prize in Literature in 1954. After releasing more works while continuously battling with the demons of depression and anxiety, Hemingway finally succumbed to suicide in 1961.

Throughout his life, Hemingway drew on his raw personal encounters as the basis for his books' plots and themes. On his journey to writing, Hemingway married four times, with each of them ending in divorce. He incorporated his feelings on his marriage on many parts of his works.

Fireside Question 1

†††

Ernest Hemingway was born in 1899. What is the prominent literary genre at the time? Who were the famous writers then?

Fireside Question 2

Hemingway's mother would often dress him in female clothes. How did Americans view gender roles in the 1890s? Where was feminism back then?

Fireside Question 3

†††

Even though he was rejected for his defective eye, Hemingway didn't give up
and applied as a Red Cross ambulance driver. What does this tell of his
character? How did his persistence help him in his career as a writer?

Fireside Question 4

†††

Hemingway sourced out his books' inspiration from the events of the war. What is the essence of war outside literature? How did it shape the world? Why do countries participate in them regardless of the bloodbath?

Fireside Question 5

At some points in his life, Hemingway was surrounded by the effects of depression in the suicide of his father-in-law and his father. Eventually, his body injuries and the continuing crises in life were enough to make him depressed. How was mental health treated at the time?

Chapter Two: Birth and Early Childhood & Education

Did You Know?

Hemingway had difficulty in writing the ending for A Farewell to Arms. He had to delay the revision of the book, whose serialization was scheduled for May 1929. But as late as April, he was still working on the ending he had already written seventeen times over.

†††

Ernest Miller Hemingway was born in Cicero (present-day Oak Park), Illinois, on July 21, 1899. His father was the physician Clarence Edmonds Hemingway, and his mother was Grace Hall, a locally famous musician. When his parents married in 1896, they first lived with Ernest Miller Hall, Grace's father; hence, their first son's name. He was the second child of six children, and the first of two sons. Hemingway lived with her sisters Marcelline, Ursula, Madelaine, Carol, and brother Leicester. The family resided in a conservative community where the parents enjoyed proper education and respect. His mother believed in the Victorian convention of not organizing children's clothes by gender. Because of this, and since Marcelline was only a year older than Hemingway, the two would often wear the same clothes, strongly resembling one another as if they're twins. His mother also kept his hair long until he was three years old, and while he was always dressed in frilly feminine clothes. She also taught her son how to play the cello, despite Hemingway's refusal to learn any musical instrument. In time, Grace's unusual parenting style contributed to her son's brewing resentment for her. Little did he know at that time that her influence, particularly in music, would help him in his future writing style, the contrapuntal structure. Even though he hated her mother, it was evident that Hemingway also shared his mother's energy and enthusiasm for the things they liked.

Each summer, the whole family traveled to Walloon Lake in Michigan, where they spent time hunting, fishing, and camping in the woods and lakes near the vicinity. Hemingway considered these times to be the most important and happy events in his youth. These activities instilled in Hemingway the life-long passion for outdoor adventures and living in isolated places.

Hemingway was predominantly educated in public schools. In 1913, Hemingway attended the Oak Park and River Forest High School, where he was involved in many sports–boxing, water polo, football, and track and field. Together with his sister Marcelline, Hemingway was also an active member of the school orchestra for two years. Even though he was very active in the extra-curricular scenes, he didn't ignore his studies. In fact, Hemingway's grades were above average, particularly in English. In his last two years in secondary education, he was a sportswriter and editor at *Trapeze,* the school's newspaper, and Tabula, their yearbook. Hemingway used the pen name, Ring Lardner Jr., inspired by Ring Lardner, the famous writer of the *Chicago Tribune.*

After four years of high school, Hemingway finally graduated in 1917. He was about to enter college when he decided to pursue a less-sheltered environment. Because of wanting to leave home, away from the conventional views of her mother, Hemingway didn't go to college and instead went to Kansas City. There, he worked as a cub reporter for *The Kansas City Star*, where he honed his writing skills for six months. In an interview later on, Hemingway admitted that his experience at his first work laid the foundations for his writing, which allowed him to appreciate the beauty of writing short sentences and short first paragraphs while using vigorous English.

Fireside Question 6

†††

When Clarence and Grace Hemingway married in 1896, they first lived with Grace's father, Ernest Miller Hall. They then named their first son to honor him. Why do some newly-formed families rely on their parents during the first years of marriage? How did this setup evolve?

Fireside Question 7

†††

Grace followed Victorian conventions and didn't differentiate her children's clothing by gender. Because of this, Hemingway and his older sister, Marcelline, would often dress the same way as if they're twins. How did this parenting style affect and influence her children? How about the relationship of the siblings with one another?

Fireside Question 8

†††

Hemingway's mother was a famous musician in their community. Why do some parents like Grace force their children to have the same interests as them? How did this contribute to the children's wellbeing while growing up?

Fireside Question 9

†††

Hemingway had an active high school life. He participated in various sports, was a member of the orchestra, and wrote for the school paper. He was also the editor for their yearbook. What is the importance of the holistic formation nurtured in a child's education?

Fireside Question 10

†††

Instead of pursuing college, Hemingway moved to Kansas and worked as a journalist instead. What made him arrive at his decision? How did journalism lay the foundation for his solid career?

Chapter Three: Professional & Career Public Adult Life

Did You Know?

Hemingway used to hate cats. When he traveled to Cuba in 1939, he met a Parisian friend who allowed his pets to eat from the table. Hemingway was disgusted by the sight, but eventually came to love them and kept dozens of cats in his Cuban residence.

†††

Journalism: While Ernest Hemingway was working as a journalist in Kansas, the United States was preparing for World War I. Like most men his age, he also wanted to be drafted for the military. However, he was rejected due to poor eyesight. To fulfill his duty of serving the country, he applied at a Red Cross recruitment, where he was deployed to Italy as an ambulance driver. In July 1918, however, Hemingway was severely injured by mortar fire when he returned from bringing supplies for the frontlines. Despite his serious wounds, he still managed to assist soldiers to safety, which earned him the Italian War Merit Cross Croce al Merito di Guerra. While recuperating in Milan for six months, he fell deeply in love with Agnes von Kurowsky. When he returned to America in January 1919, Agnes didn't join him and instead confessed that she was already engaged to an Italian officer.

U returning home from Italy, Hemingway couldn't live at home without a job. He then went on a fishing and camping trip with some high school friends when a family friend offered him a Toronto job. Hemingway accepted right away and immediately began as a freelance writer for the Toronto Star Weekly. Months later, he moved to Chicago and worked as an associate editor at Cooperative Commonwealth, where he met the famous novelist Sherwood Anderson. In 1921, Hemingway was then hired as a foreign correspondent for Paris by the Toronto Star.

In Paris, Hemingway was mentored by novelist Gertrude Stein, who also became the godmother of his first son. She introduced him to the artists and writers of the "Lost Generation." Hemingway also met poet Ezra Pound, and they maintained a strong friendship. For his work, Hemingway filed more than 80 stories for the Toronto newspaper, including coverage of the Greco-Turkish War.

In WWII, Hemingway was a correspondent during the liberation of Paris. He also became a de facto leader of a small village militia in Rambouillet. He also covered the Battle of Hurtgen Forest and the Battle of the Bulge, despite being ill. He was awarded the Bronze Star for his bravery during WWII.

Authorship: In 1923, Hemingway returned to Toronto, where he published his first book Three Stories and Ten Poems. Two years later, he then published In Our Time, a collection of short stories. Earlier, Hemingway met F. Scott

Fitzgerald when he published The Great Gatsby. Hemingway liked the masterpiece and decided his next book to be a novel like his.

In October 1926, Hemingway published The Sun Also Rises after eight weeks of writing the draft. It shared the story of the post-war generation and was considered one of Hemingway's greatest works. The same year, he also published The Torrents of Spring: A Romantic Novel in Honor of the Passing of a Great Race as a parody to Dark Laughter by Sherwood Anderson.

Hemingway released his next novel, A Farewell to Arms, in September 1928. The story was set in WWI Italy. Many agreed that it showed complexities not present in his first novel and that the book established his name as a major American novelist.

After several years of releasing non-novel works, Hemingway finally returned to the genre with To Have and Have Not in 1937, his only novel in the 1930s. The story follows the main character Harry Morgan, a fishing boat captain in Florida.

The same year, Hemingway returned to the warzone for the Spanish Civil War as a NANA correspondent. He wrote his only play, The Fifth Column, when French forces bombarded Madrid. Hemingway also witnessed with his own eyes the Battle of the Ebro in 1938.

Hemingway began writing For Whom the Bell Tolls after being inspired by his third wife, Martha Gellhorn. He wrote the manuscript while traveling to Cuba, Wyoming, and Idaho. The book was published in 1940 and was set during the Spanish Civil War. It sold more than half a million copies and became his first Pulitzer Prize-nominated work.

After many years of being an "out of business writer," Hemingway released Across the River and into the Trees he wrote in Cuba during a series of fights with Mary Welsh. The negative reviews of the book prompted him to write his next major work, The Old Man and the Sea, published in 1952. The book made Hemingway's popularity spread across countries, earning him the Pulitzer Prize the same year.

Besides fiction novels, Hemingway also released memoirs and other non-fiction books. Inspired by Spain's bullfighting sport, Hemingway began writing for another book in mid-1929. Death in the Afternoon was released in 1932, a non-fiction book explaining the ceremony and traditions of the sport. In 1933, Hemingway and Pauline Pfeiffer traveled to Africa, where he wrote Green Hills of Africa (published in 1935). The nonfiction book was an account of the trip.

Hemingway also left a lot of unpublished works. In 1946, Hemingway began working on The Garden of Eden, which was published posthumously in 1986. In 1956, after discovering his trunks from 1928, he began writing his memoir, A Moveable Feast (published in 1964). At the same time, he also wrote True at First Light and Islands in the Seams and added more chapters to The Garden of Eden. In 1959, he was commissioned to write The Dangerous Summer, a nonfiction book about the rivalry of famous Spanish bullfighters. The book was published in 1985.

Personal Life: Hemingway met Hadley Richardson, his first wife, in Chicago when she visited his roommate's sister. She was eight years his senior, but the two of them instantly clicked. After a few months of correspondence, they married and traveled to Europe. They lived in Paris. When it was clear that their marriage was already deteriorating, the two agreed to divorce. They split their possessions, and she received the proceeds from The Sun Also Rises.

Hemingway met Pauline Pfeiffer, his second wife, in Austria when revising The Sun Also Rises. The two had an affair while he was still with Richardson. They married five months after Hemingway's divorce with Richardson. They moved back to America and lived in Key East. After nine years of marriage, Hemingway and Pfeiffer divorced after a slow and painful separation.

Martha Gellhorn was also a journalist when Hemingway met her in Key East in 1937. She joined him in Cuba after he crossed to the country aboard his boat Pilar. The two got married in 1940 in Cheyenne, Wyoming. They spent their summers in Idaho and traveled to Cuba during winters. After five years, they separated and divorced after Gellhorn claimed to have been "bullied" by him.

Hemingway met Mary Welsh in London in 1944 while he was still with Gellhorn. After three meetings, he finally asked her hand in marriage, but she only agreed to marry him in 1946. In Paris, two visited Pablo Picasso and Gertrude Stein when he eventually forgave the latter. Welsh suffered a miscarriage because of an ectopic pregnancy.

Hemingway and Welsh stayed in Venice for several months in 1948. There, he fell in love with the 19-year-old Italian noble and poet Adriana Ivancich. The love affair was the inspiration behind Across the River and Into the Trees.

Death: Due to the accumulated severe injuries inflicted on his body, Hemingway's physical health began to deteriorate. Moreover, he fell into depression. In April 1961, after being released from the Mayo Clinic for electroconvulsive therapy (ECT), Welsh found him holding a shotgun in the kitchen. She immediately called his doctor, who sedated him and brought him to the hospital. Once he was released at the end of June, he returned to his home. Two days after, in the early morning of July 2, Hemingway went into his basement filled with guns and took out his favorite one. He then went upstairs to the front entrance foyer and shot himself.

Welsh initially reported that Hemingway "accidentally" killed himself. She retracted her statement five years later and confessed that Hemingway died of suicide.

Fireside Question 11

†††

Hemingway was mentored by Stein and had been friends with other famous writers such as Anderson and Fitzgerald. What is the importance of establishing relationships with other authors? How did these connections help Hemingway's career?

Fireside Question 12

†††

Throughout his life, Hemingway had many wives and affairs. Why did his marriages fail? What does this tell of Hemingway's capability to handle relationships with women?

Fireside Question 13

†††

Hemingway published both fiction and nonfiction books. Why is it important for authors to explore other genres? Did all of his books gain equal success? Which genre did he primarily excel in?

Fireside Question 14

†††

While writing his books, Hemingway often traveled. What is the significance of travels in his writing career? How did the different sceneries and cultures influence his books?

Fireside Question 15

†††

Hemingway was challenged by the negative reviews of Across the River and Into the Trees. He then wrote The Old Man and the Sea, which he claimed to his best. What is the essence of his "failure" in this context? Which factors contribute to the negative book reception? Did the latter's publication erase the inferior quality of the former?

Chapter Four: Main Difficulties Overcame in Life & Main Accomplishments and Achievements

Did You Know?

After his death, Hemingway's wife, Mary Welsh, retrieved his collection of thousands of books from the Cuban government in 1964. She then offered the Hemingway papers to the JFK Presidential Library and Museum through Jacqueline Kennedy.

††††

Main Difficulties in Life

Body Injuries: In many parts of his active life, Ernest Hemingway obtained severe injuries in his head, his knee, and other body parts. He got the first one in Italy while on duty as an ambulance driver. Hemingway was also seriously injured in his Paris bathroom, leaving a permanent scar on his forehead. In 1930, he broke his arm in a car accident on his way home after bringing his friend Dos Passos to the Billings, Montana train station. He suffered a compound spiral fracture which gave him intense pain for several months. During WWII, Hemingway had another car accident where he was brought to a hospital in London with a concussion. In 1945, he suffered a car accident for the third time, where he smashed his knee and sustained another deep forehead wound. By this time, he was also suffering from headaches, hypertension, weight problems, and diabetes. Much of his health problems were a result of his heavy drinking for many years and previous accidents. In 1954, Hemingway and Welsh were involved in two plane crashes. First was during a chartered flight to Congo, and the second happened the next day when their plane–bound for Entebbe for medical care–exploded at take-off. He suffered burns and a serious concussion that leaked cerebral fluid in his brain. The accidents result in the physical deterioration that followed Hemingway to the last of his days. However, he became a much heavier drinker to combat the painful injuries. Despite the many accidents in his life, Hemingway continued his work as a passionate journalist and exemplary author.

Mental Health: Besides physical deterioration, Hemingway's mental health was also affected by the events in his life. During his first marriage with Richardson, his father-in-law committed suicide. Later on, his father suffered the same fate. His father's death devastated Hemingway–he wrote for him earlier and the letter arrived a few minutes after he took his life. At the time, Hemingway commented, "I'll probably go the same way." His accumulated injuries have also taken their toll on his mental health. Towards the end of his life, he was devoured by paranoia for his safety. Additionally, the death of his literary friends made him lonely. After his death, it was found that he suffered from a hereditary disease that caused his mental deterioration.

Main Achievements in Life and Legacy

Hemingway's books left their marks in literature forever. Besides his Pulitzer (1953) and Nobel (1954) trophies and the millions of books sold, his most important prize can be found in the legacy he left. Even if his genre was fiction, he heavily drew on his life experiences for the stories of his books. He was proclaimed by the greatest writers such as Scott Fitzgerald and James Joyce as "the next great American novelist." His style was something his predecessors and successors avoided, making him one of the few unique authors in his right. Hemingway became the bastion and popularizer of the war novel during the post-war generation.

Even after his death, he received various tributes ranging from celestial planets to restaurants named in his honor. In 1977, the International Imitation Hemingway Competition, an annual writing competition paying mock homage to Hemingway, was established. The Hemingway Foundation was established in 1965 by Mary Welsh, and in 1980, scholars formed the Hemingway Society. Numerous literary awards were also created in his honor: the PEN Award and the Hemingway Award.

Hemingway was inducted into the Chicago Literary Hall of Fame in 2012. Some of his residences were converted into museums for the public. In April 2021, a six-hour life documentary with his name as the title was shown on the Public Broadcasting System.

Most of Hemingway's notable works were adapted into films, plays, and television series. He had also inspired a plethora of writers with his literary style, attitude, and overall perspective of life.

Hemingway was inducted into the Chicago Literary Hall of Fame in 2012. Some of his residences were converted into museums for the public. In April 2021, a six-hour life documentary with his name as the title was shown on the Public Broadcasting System.

Most of Hemingway's notable works were adapted into films, plays, and television series.

Fireside Question 16

†††

Hemingway experienced many accidents in his life that gave him severe injuries. What was his general outlook for body injuries as far as his career is concerned? Why was he prone to accidents?

Fireside Question 17

†††

Being a heavy drinker resulted in many unfortunate events in Hemingway's life. Why do people become addicted to alcohol? How did his alcoholism affect his works and his popularity?

Fireside Question 18

†††

In 1954, Hemingway and Welsh suffered two successive plane crashes. The first plane struck an abandoned utility pole before it crash-landed. The second one exploded at take-off. What was the quality of aircraft (in general) back then?

Fireside Question 19

†††

Hemingway's legacy can still be felt in the present day. How did he shape American literature? Why do many people regard him as one of the best authors?

Fireside Question 20

†††

His life's documentary was aired only recently. What is the significance of publicizing the events in his life? Why did it take many decades for such full-length narration?

Chapter Five: Conclusion

Did You Know?

In his final years, Hemingway behaved similarly to his father before killing himself. He later found out that, like his father, he also had hereditary hemochromatosis. It caused the excessive accumulation of iron in tissues, causing physical and mental deterioration. Two of his siblings also killed themselves.

†††

Ernest Hemingway was an explorer throughout his life–be it in the battlefield, the wilderness, the sea, or even inside his own literary world. He was often portrayed as an "action man" whose machismo commanded confidence and authority, but he was shy in reality. His intelligence and educational upbringing were so diverse that they must have been confused when ordinary men got to experience it. But Hemingway didn't. Instead, he weaved through the various perspectives supplied by his family and education and applied them in his life. The fact that he didn't let his poor sight stop him from serving his country was enough proof of his competent nature–always wanting for the best.

Behind the handsome man whose smiles can captivate those who saw it lies a pattern of failed marriages and relationships. Those who have studied him concluded that Hemingway did not know what he wanted–he wanted everything and nothing at the same time. He coped with this crisis through writing, and his natural talent for writing made fame replaced the temporary ghosts of his life. However, the same fame that the man enjoyed began to haunt him later on. Coupled with the frustrations from the declining physical body, he eventually gave in to the inner demons of depression.

Regardless, Hemingway left many lasting contributions to literature–writing styles that inspired numerous writers after him.

Attention: Get Your Free Gift Now

Every <u>purchase</u> now comes with a FREE Bonus Gift

2020 Top 5 Fireside Books of the Year

(New-York Times Bestsellers, USA Today & more)

<u>Get it now here:</u>

<u>Scan QR Code to Download Free Gift</u>

Printed in Great Britain
by Amazon

64568572R00028